GREAT EXIT PROJECTS ON THE
CIVIL WAR
AND
RECONSTRUCTION

GREAT SOCIAL STUDIES EXIT PROJECTS™

GREAT EXIT PROJECTS ON THE
CIVIL WAR
AND
RECONSTRUCTION

Alana Benson

rosen publishing's
rosen
central®

New York

Published in 2020 by The Rosen Publishing Group, Inc.
29 East 21st Street, New York, NY 10010

First Edition

Cataloging-in-Publication Data

Names: Benson, Alana, author.
Title: Great exit projects on the Civil War and Reconstruction / Alana Benson.
Description: New York : Rosen Publishing, 2020. | Series: Great social studies exit projects | Audience: Grades 5–8. | Includes bibliographical references and index.
Identifiers: ISBN 9781499440331 (library bound) | ISBN 9781499440355 (pbk.)
Subjects: LCSH: Reconstruction (U.S. history, 1865–1877)—Juvenile literature. | United States—History—Civil War, 1861–1865—Juvenile literature.
Classification: LCC E468.B478 2019 | DDC 973.7—dc23

Manufactured in the United States of America

CONTENTS

The United States of America: the idea is all in the name. All of the fifty states, from the White Mountains of New Hampshire to the rolling green hills of Virginia, from the coasts of California to the fields of Iowa, are part of a greater whole because they are *united*. However, it wasn't always this way. While the states are united, there can be some pretty big differences from state to state. Every region has its own quirks. In some areas of the North, people might walk and talk faster. In the South, life might slow down a bit. From the fried chicken and grits of the South to the bagels and deep-dish pizza of the North, each state has its own personality.

These differences were not always so simple. In the 1800s, states had major disagreements about big issues. They disagreed about how big of a role the government should play, and they disagreed about what issues states should be able to decide on for themselves. Most of all, they disagreed about whether slavery should be legal. Slavery has existed for most of human history in some form. Slavery had existed in America since the 1600s, from the time people from Africa were captured, brought to the New World, forced to work for nothing, and treated as property instead of human beings. Only 4 to 6 percent of captured Africans, however, were taken to America; most crossed the Middle Passage and were taken to Brazil and then to the Caribbean.

President Abraham Lincoln's election, rising tensions between the states, and differing ideas about the morality of owning slaves led to the American Civil War. This war lasted from 1861 to 1865, and though the exact number is in dispute,

Studying the Civil War shouldn't be boring. Creating an exit project relates history to real-world topics. If the topic seems uninteresting at first, find a way to make it fascinating.

at least 620,000 people died, with some estimates as high as 750,000. These numbers were catastrophic and forever altered the American landscape—especially in the South. After the Civil War, a period of Reconstruction, the process of rebuilding the South, lasted from 1865 to 1877. Reconstruction was wrought with racial tensions and struggling legislation—a time that saw both laws to help black Americans gain equality and the rise of overt racism.

The period of the Civil War and Reconstruction was complex and affected every aspect of life for the people who lived through it. The consequences of the war stretch through history to the modern day. Developing exit projects, or projects based on the accumulation of knowledge on one topic, is an excellent way to analyze complex historical periods like the Civil War and Reconstruction. Exit projects, which can be used as part of project-based learning (PBL), offer a way to engage with history and other topics through investigation and research. The projects in this book are meant to be used as models. Project-based learning is best utilized through individual thought and questioning. So use these projects as a jumping-off point, but know that they are most effective when they incorporate independent questions and ideas. What perspectives still need to be uncovered? What voices from the American Civil War need to be heard, and what stories need to be told? All of these questions and more are waiting to be explored.

RUMBLINGS OF WAR

Before the Civil War, many people believed that slavery was wrong and should be outlawed. Many of these people lived in the northern half of the United States. The majority of the people who believed slavery should be allowed lived in the southern half. This geographic divide was not just coincidence: most of the South's economy was based on agriculture, especially growing cotton. Southern plantations used slave labor so much that their economy became dependent on it. The North was more industrialized and did not depend on slave labor the way the South did.

In the mid-1800s, discontent was rising among Americans, especially in the South, about the state of their country. The Industrial Revolution had changed the landscape of the North decades prior, bringing factories and employing skilled workers. In fact, 90 percent of the skilled workers in the United States lived in the North. Not only that, but the North's population vastly outnumbered the South's—which included slaves—by almost double. The North had railroad networks, access to naval resources, and almost 70 percent of the nation's capital. All in all, the North was far better equipped to handle the war to come.

New states were also being added to the relatively new nation. Southern states, for fear of being outnumbered, wanted to be sure that these new states (like Missouri) would

Abraham Lincoln led the United States through the Civil War. He remains one of the most celebrated presidents in American history.

be slave states. This would guarantee that their interests would continue to be considered. The South argued that they had a right to secede, to hold slaves, and to not have to follow federal orders blindly. They believed that the states knew how to best govern themselves, rather than have heavy-handed oversight from Washington, DC.

These tensions came to a head with the election of Abraham Lincoln as president in 1860. Starting with South Carolina, Southern states started to secede, or leave the Union. They wanted to create their own country, called the Confederacy.

QUESTION 1 HOW DID THE CHANGING ECONOMIES OF BOTH THE NORTH AND THE SOUTH CREATE A CLIMATE FOR THE NORTH TO PROSPER AND THE SOUTH TO DECLINE IN THE LEAD-UP TO THE CIVIL WAR? HOW DID THE ECONOMIC FACTOR AFFECT THE RESENTMENTS ALREADY FELT BY MANY IN THE SOUTH?

Inventions like the cotton gin as well as shifting priorities made states face a choice. According to historian Christopher Hamner at TeachingHistory.org:

> **Given the cotton gin's effects on the spread of large-scale cotton agriculture and the resultant growth in the institution of slavery in the first half of the nineteenth century, it is difficult to portray its introduction as anything other than a disaster from the perspective of enslaved African Americans.**

For the enslaved people in America, the outlook was bleak. Technological advancements did not lead to a better quality of life for them. The economic strategy of the South demanded their enslavement.

In the South, the decision was on secession, and states were picking sides. The election of President Lincoln made tensions peak. South Carolina responded by seceding, and it was followed by ten other states. These states banded together to form the Confederate States of America and declared themselves a sovereign country.

THE COTTON GIN

The South had a mainly agricultural economy, where growing crops was the main source of income. Crops like corn, apples, tobacco, and especially cotton flourished in the sun of the South. King Cotton, as it was referred to, sustained many farmers and plantations. One invention in particular helped cotton expand in a way that affected everything from individual slaves' workloads to massive economic change. In 1794, Eli Whitney invented the cotton gin. This machine made it so slaves and other workers did not have to pick out the cotton seeds from the rest of the plant by hand. This mechanization made it so cotton fabric could be produced faster and for less money, which dropped the price of cotton and made it more available. This also increased the demand for slave labor, tightening the South's grip on their belief that slavery was necessary for their own survival.

PROJECT 1
PORTFOLIO PREDICTIONS

Heading into the Civil War, the North and South had different economic resources and advantages. Pick either the North or the South and use various primary source materials to create an economic portfolio for the pre–Civil War era.

Working in groups can provide challenges, but it can also create a better project. Hearing different perspectives and ideas can help lead to the best possible outcome.

- Using the website https://www.nps.gov/civilwar/facts.htm, research the region's economic health. How many people live in your region? How much revenue, or money, does it create? How many workers does it use? If you are profiling the South, how many slaves are there?

- Does this region rely on various industries to create revenue? Research the industries in the region, the products they produce, the percentage of profit from those industries, and those industries' requirements in terms of equipment and labor. Using this information, put together an economic portfolio that discusses your predictions for the Civil War. Will the region you are profiling be able to financially support itself? Ask questions like, "How does the cost of cotton affect the price of soldiers' uniforms?" and "How will my region's industries help fight the war?"

• Create at least two charts or graphs to help illustrate the region's economic portfolio.

QUESTION 2 COUPLED WITH RISING ECONOMIC TENSIONS, HOW DID CERTAIN LAWS HELP SPARK THE CONFLICT THAT WOULD TURN INTO THE CIVIL WAR?

The Missouri Compromise was a law passed in 1820 in an attempt to soothe the tensions between the North and the South, although it ended up aggravating them instead. This law admitted Missouri, a brand new state, into the Union as a slave state, while Maine was named a non-slave state. It also drew an imaginary line at a certain latitude and stated that any territory above that line was "free," meaning that residents of those territories could not own slaves. After much debate, divisiveness, and amending, the Missouri Compromise was repealed by the Kansas-Nebraska Act of 1854. This act stated that the people of Kansas and Nebraska should be able to decide for themselves whether or not they wanted to allow slavery in their state. Unfortunately, people were in such disagreement that an attempt at an election ended in several bouts of violence, termed "Bleeding Kansas." These smaller skirmishes resulted in the deaths of about fifty-six people, which further inflamed rising tensions.

PROJECT 2
OUTLINING THE CONFLICT

Both the Missouri Compromise and the Kansas-Nebraska Act were attempts at negotiations between the North and the South. While their intentions may have been to soothe hostilities, looking back through history, we now see that they just aggravated both sides. Create a map that depicts either the Missouri Compromise or the Kansas-Nebraska Act to show these areas in their various stages of conflict.

As new states entered the Union, it became necessary to decide whether or not they would be slave or "free" states.

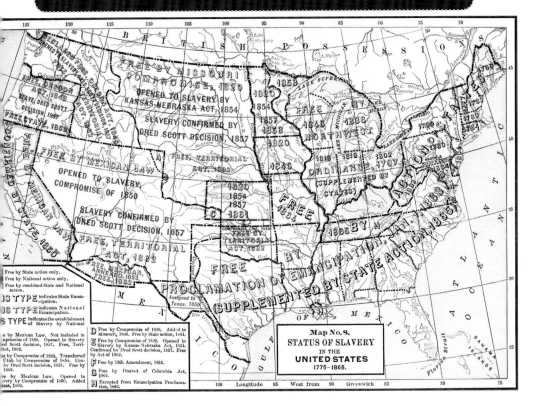

- Examine the primary documents of either the Missouri Compromise or the Kansas-Nebraska Act. You can find transcripts of both at ourdocuments.gov, an extension website run by the National Archives.
- Print out and read through the primary documents, highlighting important sections. Think about what these laws were trying to accomplish and how they were trying to appease both sides.
- Research the consequences of these documents. What happened specifically because these laws were enacted?
- Using your knowledge of the Missouri Compromise and the Kansas-Nebraska Act, draw a map of the region affected by one of these laws. Use different colors of highlighter to mark areas where slavery was legal and where it was outlawed. Then indicate areas of conflict with their dates and the number of casualties.
- Drawing on your research and the map you have created, write a one-page essay on how the Missouri Compromise or the Kansas-Nebraska Act contributed to the outbreak of the Civil War.

CHAPTER TWO

A COUNTRY DIVIDED

President Lincoln was elected in November of 1860. The night he was elected, South Carolina seceded. Several Southern states followed suit to form the Confederacy. When President Lincoln was inaugurated, or formally brought into the office as the president, he arrived in Washington, DC, in disguise. Things were so tense between the North and the South that Lincoln was the target of several assassination attempts. Soon, these tensions escalated to war with the attack on Fort Sumter on April 12, 1861.

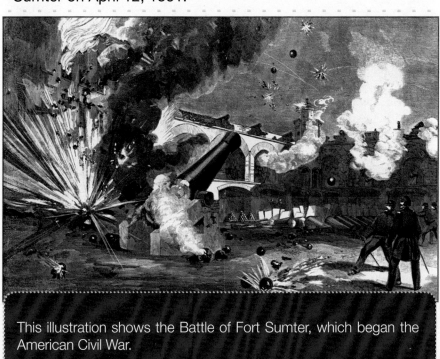

This illustration shows the Battle of Fort Sumter, which began the American Civil War.

In the months leading up to the battle, the Southern states had begun ramping up their military forces. In South Carolina, a Confederate general named P. T. Beauregard had started building up his forces around Charleston Harbor. In response, a Union commander, Major Robert Anderson, moved his troops from the vulnerable Fort Moultrie to the impressive Fort Sumter, located on an island in the middle of Charleston Harbor. Fort Sumter was better fortified and had a more strategic position. To the Confederate side, this meant war. The Confederate general Beauregard sent the Union major Anderson the following message, stating that his troops would fire if Anderson did not surrender.

April 11, 1861
Major Anderson,

The Government of the Confederate States has hitherto forborne from any hostile demonstration against Fort Sumter, in the hope that the Government of the United States, with a view to the amicable adjustment of all questions between the two Governments, and to avert the calamities of war, would voluntarily evacuate it.

There was reason at one time to believe that such would be the course pursued by the Government of the United States, and under that impression my Government has refrained from making any demand for the surrender of the fort. But the Confederate States can no longer delay assuming actual possession of a fortification commanding the entrance of one of their harbors, and necessary to its defense and security.

I am ordered by the Government of the Confederate States to demand the evacuation of Fort Sumter. My aides,

Colonel Chestnut and Captain Lee, are authorized to make such demand of you. All proper facilities will be afforded for the removal of yourself and command, together with company arms and property, and all private property, to any post in the United States which you may select. The flag which you have upheld so long and with so much fortitude, under the most trying circumstances, may be saluted by you on taking it down.

Colonel Chestnut and Captain Lee will, for a reasonable time, await your answer.

I am, sir, very respectfully, your obedient servant,

G. T. Beauregard

But Major Anderson would not surrender. He sent the following brief response to General Beauregard.

April 11, 1861
Brigadier-General Beauregard,

I have the honor to acknowledge the receipt of your communication demanding the evacuation of this fort, and to say, in reply thereto, that it is a demand with which I regret that my sense of honor, and of my obligations to my Government, prevent my compliance. Thanking you for the fair, manly, and courteous terms proposed, and for the high compliment paid me.

I am, general, very respectfully, your obedient servant,

Robert Anderson

Early in the morning of April 12, 1861, the Confederates fired the first shot, which exploded over Fort Sumter. The Union troops awaited daylight to fire back. The Civil War had begun.

QUESTION 3 WHY DID UNION COMMANDER MAJOR ANDERSON MOVE HIS TROOPS TO FORT SUMTER? WHAT GEOGRAPHICAL AND MILITARISTIC ADVANTAGES DID THAT FORT HAVE OVER FORT MOULTRIE, THE PLACE THEY HAD PREVIOUSLY OCCUPIED?

While Fort Sumter was better fortified, Major Anderson and his men faced bombardment on all sides and quickly ran out of supplies. Since they were surrounded, supply ships could not get to the Union side. In addition to food, they were also running out of ammunition. Major Anderson attempted to conserve the ammunition they had while also commanding his troops to avoid using the most powerful cannons in the fort because they would be exposed to Confederate fire.

After only thirty-four hours of fighting, Major Anderson was forced to surrender. This was the first win for the Confederates, but no one knew how long the war would drag on. Most people thought it would be over fairly quickly. While Fort Sumter was the first fight, the real battles came later. And, unfortunately, no other battle would end with zero casualties.

PROJECT 3
BATTLE PLANS

Both Major Anderson of the Union army and General Beauregard of the Confederate army had to make serious decisions within a

Using historical maps and your knowledge of history, you can re-create maps of important events like the Battle of Fort Sumter in order to better understand what occurred.

thirty-four-hour period. Using primary sources and other reliable sources, draw a map of what the battle looked like. Include Fort Sumter, Fort Moultrie, the harbor, the coastline, and any other sites of importance. Include lots of details, like what soldiers were stationed where and in which forts, and the weapons they were using.

- Find historical maps online to help make the map as accurate as possible.
- Read "1.3 Fort Sumter," a lesson featured on learnnc .com, a website run by the University of North Carolina, and take notes on the details of the forts. Use these

notes to draw cannon ports, gunrooms, and barracks. Be sure to label as much as possible. Draw a key and a compass to keep the map organized. Use arrows to indicate cannon fire.

- To accompany the map, write three paragraphs to discuss both sides' battle plans and whether you think either of them made a mistake. If you were in their shoes, using your knowledge of the geography of the area and the amount of resources available, what would you have done differently?

QUESTION 4 WHO ARE THE MAJOR MILITARY FIGURES FROM THE AMERICAN CIVIL WAR? WHAT DOES AMERICA REMEMBER ABOUT THESE INDIVIDUALS—AND ARE OUR MEMORIES ACCURATE? IN OTHER WORDS, WHAT DID HISTORY FORGET ABOUT THESE PEOPLE?

Ulysses S. Grant. Robert E. Lee. "Stonewall" Jackson. These are household names, even today. Each of these people played a significant role in the Civil War. Ulysses S. Grant led the Union army to victory and later became a United States president. Robert E. Lee led the Confederate army and eventually surrendered. Jackson was Lee's right-hand man and a brilliant strategist.

War is full of tough choices, and those in charge often bear the brunt of the responsibility. For that reason, the memoirs and letters of these individuals often reflect that burden. Most of those men were responsible, perhaps indirectly, for the deaths of thousands of soldiers during the Civil War. How did they justify their actions? Each believed they were fighting for a worthy cause, but at some point they probably questioned whether or not they were doing the right thing.

PROJECT 4
SHIFTING FIGURES

Public perception about military figures in the Civil War has changed over the years. For example, many Confederate generals were praised for their dedication to the South immediately following the Civil War. One hundred years later, as the civil rights movement further exposed both the racist ideology that underpinned slavery and how that racism continued in the modern day, public perception about Confederate figures shifted. Choose a major military figure from the American Civil War and research changing perceptions of that figure, using historical and contemporary documents. Then create a presentation using the information you have gathered to show how people have responded differently to that military leader over time.

Robert E. Lee led the Confederate troops during the Civil War. Lee's role in defending slavery continues to cause controversy today with activists arguing his statues should be taken down.

- Research the military figure you have chosen, including his background and how he became involved in the military.
- Find primary sources from the Civil War era that discuss people's perceptions of the individual you are researching. If possible, find letters, articles, or speeches written by the military figure himself.
- Now, research documents written about this person after his lifetime. How did perceptions change about this figure? Why do you think public perception changed?
- In recent years, activists have called for statues of Confederate leaders, as well as monuments and streets named after them, to be removed, given their support of slavery and the damage such racism has inflicted on generations of African Americans. Were there calls to remove monuments of the person you are researching? Find statements given by activists about why they think these figures should not be commemorated.
- Finally, think about your own perception of this figure. Using your research and your own informed opinion, create a presentation using PowerPoint or another similar tool to express how opinions have changed about this person over time. You can use images of the person and primary source documents in your presentation.

QUESTION 5 WHAT DID LIFE LOOK LIKE FOR EVERYDAY PEOPLE DURING THE AMERICAN CIVIL WAR?

Not all the best stories come from the best-known figures. Some of the most striking accounts of the Civil War come from people who lived through it, like slaves, straining for news of the war while they were still forced to work, and field nurses, whose worlds were previously constricted to the house and who were now saving lives and seeing grisly injuries. There were also accounts written by native peoples, many of whom served in the Civil War for either the Union or Confederate side, and parents whose children had gone off to fight. While these voices do not get as much recognition as military generals, they may be even more important in telling us how regular people experienced the war.

PRIVATE WAKEMAN

This is an excerpt from a letter written by Private Sarah Wakeman, a nineteen-year-old woman who posed as a man and enlisted in the Union army.

When I go there I saw some soldiers. They wanted I should enlist and so I did. I got 100 and 52$ in money. I enlisted for 3 years or soon [as] discharged. All the money I send you I want you should spend it for the family in clothing or something to eat. Don't save it for me for I can get all the money I want. If I ever return I shall have money enough for my self and to divide with you …

I want to drop all old affray [fights] and I want you to do the same and when I come home we will be good friends as ever.

Good-by for the present.
Sarah Rosetta Wakeman

PROJECT 5
A DAY IN THE LIFE

Write a journal entry from the perspective of an everyday individual living through the Civil War. Include as much detail as possible.

- Use primary sources for the majority of the research. Find at least three letters or diary entries from a similar perspective the letter will be written from. For example, if you plan to write from the perspective of a mother whose

The individuals who kept journals during the war probably never thought students would be reading them and drawing inspiration from them hundreds of years later!

child is fighting in the war on the Union side, find primary sources from a parent on the Union side, a neighbor of a parent, or a sibling of the child who is away.

- You can use the University of Maryland's guide, entitled "American Civil War: Resources in Special Collections," to help find primary source books, and https://www.nps .gov/civilwar to find online resources about the Civil War, including maps and profiles of those who lived through the war, offered through the National Park Service.
- Write the journal entry around the time of a major event or battle in the war. How did your individual hear about it? What is their opinion? Are they optimistic or pessimistic about the war?
- Use evidence the individual would have had (not your own knowledge of the future) and make two informed predictions about the war. Even if your predictions are historically wrong, they should be informed by the information this individual had—perhaps a primary source newspaper article they would have read.

THE MAN, THE HAT, THE LEGEND

President Abraham Lincoln was a striking figure: he stood over 6 feet (1.83 meters) tall, with a strong profile, and he often wore his unforgettable top hat. While Lincoln became an extraordinary man, he experienced a very typical childhood for the time. Born in a log cabin in Kentucky, Lincoln grew up mostly in Indiana and received an estimated eighteen months of education. He eventually became a lawyer through self-study, which led him to politics.

We remember Lincoln as being the great president who freed the slaves, but he did not necessarily believe that black and white Americans were equal. President Lincoln wanted to abolish, or end, slavery in the United States, but that conclusion took him a little while to come to. While he believed slavery was inherently wrong, he was not necessarily sure what to do with black Americans once they had been freed. Before he became president, Lincoln delivered the Peoria speech, in which he stated that his first impulse, if all earthly power was his, was to "free all the slaves, and send them to Liberia,—to their own native land." He admitted that this would both be impossible and a death sentence for the people he would be sending back. Later in that speech, he pondered what the

The 1864 oil painting *The First Reading of the Emancipation Proclamation of President Lincoln,* by Francis Carpenter, aims to re-create the moment when slaves were set free in the Confederacy.

fate of freed slaves should be by saying, "Free them, and make them politically and socially, our equals? My own feelings will not admit of this; and if mine would, we well know that those of the great mass of white people will not … We can not, then, make them equals."

On January 1, 1863, Abraham Lincoln announced the Emancipation Proclamation, an executive order that freed all slaves held in the Confederate States. It also allowed black Americans to fight in the Union army. This order did have some limitations, though. For example, it did not extend to slaves who lived in border states, like Delaware and Maryland, that remained in the Union. Despite its limitations, the Emancipation Proclamation paved the way to set millions of people free.

HARRIET TUBMAN: SOLDIER AND SPY

You may know that Harriet Tubman escaped slavery and became a conductor on the Underground Railroad, but did you know she was also a spy? Tubman's role in history did not stop at freeing slaves. She also served as a soldier in the Civil War—a role she rarely gets credit for. In 1863, Tubman, commanding a team of 150 black soldiers, attacked slaveholders in the Combahee River Raid and freed over 750 slaves. She also worked as a cook and cleaner during the war. Despite her heroic and selfless actions, the federal government in the North did not compensate her for her military service for thirty years. Over one hundred years after her death, however, the US government finally decided to honor her and put her face on the $20 bill.

QUESTION 6 WHY DID ABRAHAM LINCOLN WAIT SO LONG—TWO YEARS AFTER THE START OF THE CIVIL WAR—TO SET AFRICAN AMERICANS FREE?

The state of the Union was fragile. The Civil War was slogging on much longer than anyone, Union or Confederate, had expected. President Lincoln needed to be strategic as he planned the future for the country. Many white Americans still supported slavery.

While they supported an immoral institution, Lincoln felt that he needed to gain their support before working to abolish slavery. He did not feel that he could grant freedom to African Americans without the full support of the Union.

According to Columbia University history professor Eric Foner, Lincoln stopped thinking about sending ex-slaves back to Africa, or even a gradual change for the country in terms of ending slavery, with the Emancipation Proclamation. The executive order was a turning point, partly because it allowed African Americans to serve in the Union army. In an interview with National Public Radio (NPR), Foner stated, "It's the black soldiers and their role which really begins as the stimulus in Lincoln's change [with regard to] racial attitudes and attitudes toward America as an interracial society in the last two years of his life." But there was still a long way to go to get African Americans the rights they deserved.

PROJECT 6
THE ECHOES OF THE EMANCIPATION PROCLAMATION

Many people view the Emancipation Proclamation as the beginning of the end of slavery. As such, it is an important document that scholars continue to study today.

- **Find the article "The Emancipation Proclamation Now" by Colleen Walsh, which is featured online in the *Harvard Gazette* from February 4, 2013.**
- **Read the article and note how the professors connect the Emancipation Proclamation to other events in history.**

- Find the text of the Thirteenth Amendment online. Think about how the Thirteenth Amendment connects to and furthered the Emancipation Proclamation.
- Write a response in the style of the professors featured in the *Harvard Gazette* piece. What echoes of the Emancipation Proclamation do you still see today? What about fifty years ago?

You can research contemporary reactions to the Emancipation Proclamation online in order to understand the impact this document had in its time—and today.

QUESTION 7 WHAT MADE THE GETTYSBURG ADDRESS SO WELL REMEMBERED? DO YOU THINK IT IS A GOOD OR BAD SPEECH? WHY?

In July of 1863, the Battle of Gettysburg claimed the lives of over 8,000 soldiers. Robert E. Lee, the leader of the Confederate side, was trying to defeat the Union Army there so his troops could advance north. On the third day of fighting, General Lee sent another general and 12,500 troops into a fatal attack in the center line of the Union army. This became Lee's undoing, and the Confederates retreated, leaving the Union victorious.

Months later, on the battlefield where so many people died, President Abraham Lincoln gave one of the most famous speeches in American history. The speech was only two minutes long—and many people mocked the president for his brief address. This short speech later became known as the Gettysburg Address.

The Gettysburg Address touched on America's Founding Fathers' principles, with Lincoln stating that America had been formed so that people could have freedom. He also noted that the fallen soldiers had made the ultimate sacrifice and that the best way to honor them was to continue the work they had died for, so they would not have died in vain.

PROJECT 7
YOUR OWN GETTYSBURG ADDRESS

The Gettysburg Address was incredibly short, but it certainly packed a punch. Using a similar format—brief, but impactful—craft a speech similar in style to the Gettysburg Address about

When delivering a speech, remember to speak more slowly than you think you need to. Lots of people accidentally speed up when they're nervous.

an issue you are passionate about today. If you need more inspiration, look at some of Lincoln's other speeches, like the House Divided speech, to get a better idea of his speaking style.

- Find the original text of the Gettysburg Address online.
- Analyze the speech and break down its major parts. What was Abraham Lincoln's main point? What tools did he use to get people to care about what he was talking about? Which lines are the most powerful, and why?
- Research an issue that is important to you. It can be a major global or national issue, like the global refugee

crisis, gun control and laws, racism in America today, or something important in your local community, like bullying in school.

- Craft a speech modeled after the Gettysburg Address on your topic. Memorize it and deliver it in class. It should be under two minutes, and while it should have no lines taken from the Gettysburg Address, it should mimic its tone.

DID YOU KNOW?

It may come as a surprise, but the Great Emancipator, President Abraham Lincoln, is enshrined as an honorary member in the Wrestling Hall of Fame. As a young man, Lincoln was an accomplished fighter. He wrestled and boxed, and he is said to have a record of one loss out of three hundred matches! His tall and lanky frame and long arms helped him not only to lock his opponents in, but to reach them from a farther range. We typically think of President Lincoln as a peaceful man, but you'd better watch out if you found yourself in the ring with him!

QUESTION 8 HOW DID ABRAHAM LINCOLN'S VIEWS ON SLAVERY AND THE RIGHTS OF AFRICAN AMERICANS CHANGE THROUGHOUT THE WAR? WHAT PERSONAL EXPERIENCES BROUGHT ABOUT CHANGES IN HIS OPINION?

Lincoln's upbringing and political career exposed him to many different types of people, from many different walks of life.

Through his letters, speeches, and support of different forms of legislation, we can observe how Lincoln's views on slavery, and then later the rights of African Americans, changed over time. Considering how his views shifted from when he was a presidential candidate, giving speeches like the Peoria speech, to enacting the Emancipation Proclamation, to the Gettysburg Address in which he emphasizes the rights of all men (notably, as women still were not viewed as citizens with equal rights) as inalienable.

PROJECT 8
LINCOLN'S CIVIC EVOLUTION

Civics is the study of the rights and duties a citizen holds within their country. Looking at the progression of President Lincoln's writings, how did his views on African Americans change, and how did that affect policy he enacted?

- Look at various brief biographies of President Lincoln. Find three quotes from him from earlier in his career, either through primary sources or through reputable biographical accounts, which reflect the views he held at that point. Find three more from the end of his career, one each from the Emancipation Proclamation or the Gettysburg Address, which show a different view.

- Compare the quotes and use them to support an argument about how President Lincoln's views changed over time. Develop your argument into a two-page argumentative paper.

- Think about the importance of civic engagement and how the morals of one person can affect a group. Based on the information you gathered on

President Lincoln's views changed over time, and his personal growth led to the moral growth of a nation.

President Lincoln's changing views, think of a modern example of a political leader who changed his or her views on an important issue.

- Research that leader's life and try to find statements they made about why they changed their opinion. What personal or political events led to their new perspective?
- Draft a two-page argumentative paper on whether you think it is better to remain steadfast in your political opinions or to change your viewpoints based on life experiences. You can draw from the research you have done and your own personal experiences.

ATLANTA TO SAVANNAH

After the Battle at Gettysburg, the Union army had the upper hand. General William T. Sherman, a Union army leader, wanted to finish off the war. After defeating Confederate general John Hood in Atlanta in 1864, he marched his army south to the seaport town of Savannah. On their way, Sherman's army did not just march—they laid utter waste to the South. They performed scorched-earth techniques, where soldiers destroy anything the enemy could use, burning the ground so crops could not grow, destroying water sources, and wrecking transportation access like roads and bridges.

It is horrifying to imagine what regular people experienced as the war invaded their lives. One researcher found 450 court-martial cases concerning rape and other

General Sherman's troops caused total destruction in the South, but he believed the war ended sooner because of their actions.

forms of sexual violence from the Civil War. Noting that most rapes and other sexual crimes go unreported—especially in the 1800s and during wartime when there are far fewer resources to help survivors—the numbers are most certainly higher. One account from the summer of 1864 told of a young African American girl named Jenny Green who had tried to find shelter with the Union army. Instead, she was raped by a lieutenant. As horrifying as it was, because of the Lieber Code, which dictated how soldiers should conduct themselves during wartime, she was able to bring him to court. For an African American girl in 1864 to bring an older, white soldier from the Union army up on charges and win in front of an all-male tribunal was revolutionary.

JEFFERSON DAVIS, THE OTHER PRESIDENT

While Lincoln was leading the Union, a man named Jefferson Davis was elected president of the Confederacy. Davis grew up in Kentucky, attended West Point Military Academy, and farmed cotton while preparing for a career in politics. As a senator before the war, Davis was a staunch and vocal advocate of slavery and states' rights, and when the Confederacy broke from the Union, he resigned. He became the president of the Confederacy in 1861. Four years later, he was captured and charged with treason. Despite this, he was never tried, and he managed to become a cultural icon to Southerners still bitter about the war. He still manages to cause controversy in modern times. In 2017, statues of Davis were taken down across the South after protests broke out. Many people disliked the idea of having monuments to people who advocated slavery, racism, and secession.

QUESTION 9 WAS GENERAL SHERMAN'S STRATEGY MORAL? WHY OR WHY NOT? HOW HAS MODERNITY AND WARFARE TODAY CHANGED OUR IDEAS ON HOW WARS SHOULD BE FOUGHT?

According to General Sherman, during the war, "There is many a boy here today who looks on war as all glory, but, boys, it is all hell." He also said, "War is cruelty, there is no use trying to reform it; the crueler it is, the sooner it will be over." While his march devastated the South, some argue that it prevented more harm over the long term by ending the war earlier. Others, however, argue that the destruction caused by Sherman and his soldiers crippled the South. Because of the way they swiftly concluded the war, they ensured that Reconstruction would be a brutal process.

General Sherman was certainly not the first general to wage war this way; however, he was the first modern general to strike at the enemy's infrastructure as a way of incapacitating them. This tactic has been used many times since then, as has the strategy of targeting civilians and food supplies. The idea of ending the war to end suffering has been used as justification since then as well, particularly in the nuclear bombing of Hiroshima during the later half of World War II. Thinking about other examples from history, can we truly justify these tactics of war?

PROJECT 9
THE MORALITY OF THE MARCH

Consider General Sherman's march across the South and the use of scorched-earth policies in wars since. Draft an argumentative

41

Argumentative essays should consider the opposition's points. To better craft a strong essay, consider what the other side would say.

essay stating your opinion that the march was or was not moral and whether these tactics should or should not be allowed during war.

- Research facts and statistics from reputable sources, such as the Civil War Trust's page on Sherman's march at https://www.civilwar.org/learn/articles/scorched-earth.
- General Sherman outlined some rules for his soldiers to follow. Find these rules online and use them to defend your argument. Did soldiers actually follow the rules Sherman set?

- Draft a two-page argumentative essay stating whether or not you believe General Sherman's march was moral. You might consider the following questions while writing your essay: How many people died? How many of those were soldiers versus civilians? How much food did the Union army take from Southerners? Did their actions force other people to starve? Do you think Sherman actually ended the war earlier than it would have ended had he not marched his army across the South? What was the extent of the damage in the cities?
- Read the article "General Sherman's Destructive Path Blazed a New Strategy" by Jay Tolson as published on the *US News* website. How were Sherman's tactics used in subsequent wars? Did this article change your mind about Sherman's scorched-earth strategy? Why or why not?
- Partner up with someone in your class who has a different opinion from you and debate whether or not Sherman's march was in fact a moral decision.

QUESTION 10 HOW DID GENERAL SHERMAN'S MARCH RESHAPE THE ECONOMIC LANDSCAPE OF THE SOUTH?

General Sherman's army was estimated to have caused over $100 million in damage—and that's in 1864 dollars. His army tore up railroad ties, heated them, and bent them around trees. They destroyed cotton gins and fields, mills, and pretty much anything else they came across. General Sherman did not just want to defeat the South—he wanted to break it.

43

General Sherman's army marched over 400 miles (643 kilometers), laying waste to almost everything in their path. The Confederate army, at this point, was in shambles. Confederate soldiers fled, some to protect their families, and others just to get out of the way of Sherman's destruction. It wasn't just General Sherman either—his soldiers had just slogged through four long years of war. In their minds, the only reason they were involved in the war at all was because of the South's inability to give up their slaves. Contempt for Southern gentry, and wealthier individuals in general, blazed through the Union army, and while they marched through the countryside, they did not hold back. General Sherman was also aware that if they were going to win against the South, they had to do it with a note of finality and leave no possibility of further rebellion to chance.

PROJECT 10
CHARTING GENERAL SHERMAN'S MARCH

Looking at maps, chart the course General Sherman took from Atlanta to Savannah. Mark the map with landmarks, battle sites, and important numbers and events. Be as creative as you can be. Use printouts of Google Earth images that show the mountain ranges, rivers, and forested areas, or create your own diorama with art supplies.

- **Use primary sources and maps to chart Sherman's path. Look at the "Map of Sherman's March to Savannah" by Hal Jespersen to get an idea of what kinds of things should be featured on your map. The map is found at http://www.ilibrarian.net/history/shermans_march_to _the_sea_map.png.**

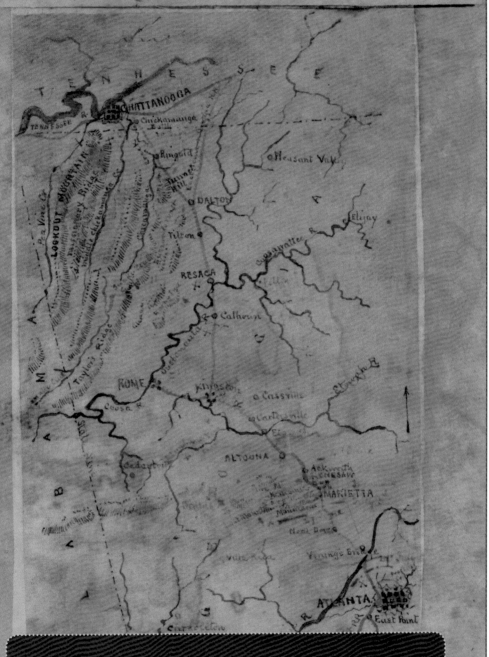

MAP SHOWING Genl. SHERMAN'S MARCH
FROM CHATTANOOGA ; ATLANTA

Using historical maps such as this one, you can chart the path that General Sherman's army took from Atlanta to Savannah.

- Mark Sherman's path and include where he broke his forces into groups and what that accomplished. Write out the numbers of casualties on both sides.

- Research the economic damage caused by Sherman's march using the scholarly article "Capital Destruction and Economic Growth: The Effects of Sherman's March, 1850–1920," by James Feigenbaum et al. What areas did his army destroy and why? What were the economic costs to the South? Be sure to include what resources the South needed that the North destroyed as part of its tactic of war.

- Write a one-page paper to accompany the map, explaining how the North's strategy affected the South economically, which in turn affected its ability to fight in the war.

CHAPTER FIVE

REBUILDING AND REMEMBERING

After General Sherman's march—and the war at large—the South was decimated. Buildings and farmlands were burned to the ground, and the South's economy was largely destroyed. After the end of the war, it was time to rebuild the South. This era became known as Reconstruction. Many people wanted

After the war, the South was destroyed. This began the period called Reconstruction, in which the South was rebuilt.

to punish the South, but President Lincoln wanted to help the healing process. His idea was to allow anyone who took an oath swearing allegiance to the Union to be given a pardon and that if only 10 percent of voters in a state supported the Union, that state could be readmitted.

Unfortunately, Lincoln would never live to see the nation heal from the war. President Lincoln was assassinated by an actor named John Wilkes Booth on April 14, 1865, just days after the war officially ended. Booth was an extremist sympathizer with the South, and believed he was chosen by God to fight for slavery. He shot the president from behind while he was watching a play at Ford's Theatre in Washington, DC. After Lincoln's death, Andrew Johnson became president. He was from the South, and he wanted to be even more sympathetic and lenient with the southern half of the nation.

FREAKY COINCIDENCES

Less than a year before the actor John Wilkes Booth assassinated President Lincoln, there was another connection between the two strangers. Booth's brother, Edwin Booth (who was also an actor, and pretty famous at the time), saved Lincoln's son Robert from falling onto a train platform. For many years it was thought to be a bit of mythology, but Robert Lincoln later recounted the incident in a letter that was then published in *Century Magazine*. He wrote:

"The train began to move, and by the motion I was twisted off my feet ... when my coat collar was vigorously seized and I was quickly pulled up and out to a secure footing on the platform. Upon turning to thank my rescuer I saw it was Edwin Booth, whose face was of course well known to me." Talk about a crazy coincidence!

The South was frustrated by the US government and took their anger out on one of the most vulnerable groups: recently freed slaves. Black codes, laws that prohibited and limited African Americans' freedoms and rights, were instituted locally in an effort to get around federal laws and any attempt at helping African Americans navigate life. To counteract these restrictions, the federal government opened schools for African American children, as well as the Freedmen's Bureau, which was an organization to help provide services like food, housing, and medical help, among other things.

Reconstruction lasted roughly until 1877, when the last federal troops were removed from the South. Much of the progress made toward equal rights was unfortunately lost after state governments took over. The South slowly recovered, but civil changes were still a long way off.

QUESTION 11 MANY HISTORIANS TRACE JIM CROW LAWS AND OTHER INSTITUTIONALIZED RACIST POLICIES BACK TO THE BLACK CODES OF RECONSTRUCTION. WHAT ECHOES OF THE ARCHAIC BLACK CODES ARE STILL PRESENT TODAY?

Losing the Civil War did not make proslavery white Southerners less racist. If anything, African Americans became a target for their anger. Black codes focused on keeping the newly freed people working on plantations for minimal wages that made it impossible for them to have any kind of mobility, whether social, economic, or otherwise. The new freedom for African Americans was looking a lot like slavery.

PROJECT 11
THE WINDING ROAD OF RACISM

Do some research on the black codes. How are these codes similar to other cases in American (or global) history when one group attempts to suppress another?

- Find three examples of specific black code laws that were enacted in the South during Reconstruction. Use primary sources or sources that lead you to primary sources like BlackPast.org. This page lists much of the legislation passed concerning African Americans.

- Trace these codes and their effects through the civil rights movement of the mid-1900s and then through to today. For each code, find an example of how restrictions enforced in the code are echoed in future laws or actions during the civil rights era and today. For example, in 1870, a miscegenation law was passed, prohibiting intermarriage between black and white people. In 1967, the US Supreme Court struck down anti-intermarriage laws across the country in the court case *Loving v. Virginia*. In 2013, a breakfast cereal company ran a commercial during the Super Bowl that featured an interracial family. The racist backlash that accompanied it was so bad that the comment section of the video online was shut down.

- For one of the three codes, connect it to a modern issue involving racism against a different racial, religious, or ethnic community, for example, the anti-Muslim sentiment spreading across Europe or the backlash

The internet is a useful research tool, but don't forget about the library! Most libraries have archival sections that will have resources the internet doesn't.

against Latin and South American immigrants coming to the United States.

- Create a poster including the information you have found and the connections you have made. Decorate the poster with historical photographs or your own illustrations. Present your poster to your class.

QUESTION 12 HOW HAVE POSTWAR ART, MOVIES, AND LITERATURE SHAPED OUR COLLECTIVE MEMORIES OF THE CIVIL WAR?

The way we remember the Civil War and Reconstruction has been curiously changed over time. In many ways, it has been romanticized. One of the most classic films of all time, *Gone with the Wind*, explores the Civil War and Reconstruction in the South. Plenty of paintings do the same, by showing the fighting and battles of the Civil War as a time of glory, rather than the bloody, destructive, and devastating war that it was.

PROJECT 12
REMEMBERING THROUGH MOVIES

Through watching and analyzing movies, figure out what was historically accurate and what was artistic choice. Films like *Gone with the Wind, Cold Mountain, Glory,* and *Lincoln* have helped shape our notions of what the Civil War and Reconstruction looked like. While some films are more accurate than others, all to some extent dramatize or romanticize the events that occurred.

- Choose a film mentioned above or another movie set in the Civil War or Reconstruction era. Watch it and take notes.
- After watching the film, go back and do some research to verify your initial reactions using some of the resources already listed in this book.
- What was accurate in this movie? What was exaggerated or fake?

Many older, classic films like *Gone with the Wind* are available for free online.

- How have any false portrayals or exaggerations in the film helped make people remember the Civil War or Reconstruction differently than how it actually occurred?
- Create a list of disparities between the film and the historical event. Using clips from the movie, present your findings to your class.

GLOSSARY

ABOLISH To end or finish.

AMERICAN CIVIL WAR The war fought between the Northern and Southern halves of the United States between 1861 and 1865, primarily over the legality of slavery.

ASSASSINATE To murder an important person for political or religious reasons.

BLACK CODES Laws that prohibited and limited black Americans' freedoms and rights. These laws were instituted locally in an effort to get around Congress's laws.

CASUALTY A person killed in a war or an accident.

CIVICS The study of the principles a person holds when it comes to citizenship, including their rights and duties as a member of a group.

CONFEDERACY Also called the Confederate States of America, this was an unrecognized country during the American Civil War created by the states that seceded from the Union.

COTTON GIN A machine invented by Eli Whitney that allowed cotton seeds to be separated from the rest of the plant mechanically, instead of by hand. The mechanization made it so cotton fabric could be produced faster and for less money.

EMANCIPATION PROCLAMATION An executive order by Abraham Lincoln that freed all slaves held in the Confederate States. This order did not free slaves in the border states of Delaware, Kentucky, Maryland, and Missouri.

INAUGURATION The process of formally inducting an elected official into office, typically used for the presidency.

KANSAS-NEBRASKA ACT An act that stated the people of Kansas and Nebraska should be able to decide for themselves whether or not they wanted to allow slavery in their state.

LIEBER CODE A set of instructions from President Abraham Lincoln on how soldiers should conduct themselves in wartime.

MIDDLE PASSAGE The part of the journey where Africans were brutally transported to the New World as part of the Atlantic slave trade.

MISSOURI COMPROMISE A law passed in 1820 that admitted Missouri as a slave state, while Maine was admitted as a non-slave state.

MORALITY A set of ideas concerning the distinction between right and wrong and good and bad.

RECONSTRUCTION The period of rebuilding the South after the American Civil War. Reconstruction lasted from 1865 to 1877.

SCORCHED-EARTH A technique of war where soldiers destroy anything the enemy could use, like burning the ground so crops cannot grow, destroying water sources, and wrecking transportation access like roads and bridges.

SECEDE To withdraw or leave.

SLAVERY An institution that forces human beings to work without pay and be treated as the property of other people.

UNDERGROUND RAILROAD A network of safe houses that helped people escape from slavery toward the North.

UNION The state of being united; during the Civil War, the Union was made up of the United States government and the twenty-five states that remained loyal to it.

FOR MORE INFORMATION

Library of Congress (LOC)
101 Independence Avenue SE
Washington, DC 20540
(202) 707-5000
Website: https://www.loc.gov
Facebook: @LibraryofCongress
Instagram and Twitter: @LibraryCongress
The Library of Congress is the research arm of the US government and has the largest library in the world. It holds one of the largest collections of Civil War documents available, including prints and photographs.

National Archives and Records Administration (NARA)
8601 Adelphi Road
College Park, MD 20740
(866) 272-6272
Website: https://www.archives.gov
Facebook: @USNationalArchives
Instagram and Twitter: @USNatArchives
The National Archives and Records Administration is the federal government's record keeper. The organization preserves important government records, such as census data and other records for soldiers who fought in the Civil War. Many of these records are available through its website.

National Park Service (NPS)
1849 C Street NW

Washington, DC 20240

(202) 208-6843

Website: https://www.nps.gov

Facebook and Instagram: @NationalParkService

Twitter: @NatlParkService

The National Park Service is a bureau of the US Department of the Interior and safeguards US national parks. As such, it maintains most of the Civil War battlefields and provides online resources about the battlefields and the conflicts that took place on them.

National Woman's Relief Corps (WRC)

(217) 522-4373

Website: womansreliefcorps.org

Email: womansreliefcorps@gmail.com

The National Woman's Relief Corps is an organization that was formed in 1883 to preserve research, documents, and records pertaining to the American Civil War. It originally served as a branch of the Grand Army of the Republic (GAR), which was an organization for Civil War veterans. The WRC also holds an annual essay contest for middle school students.

Our Documents

Website: https://www.ourdocuments.gov

Email: info@nationalhistoryday.org

Our Documents is an initiative created by the National Archives and National History Day, among others. It provides tools for teachers of American history and one hundred milestone documents for students. It also organizes history-related student competitions.

Project Gutenberg Literary Archive Foundation (PGLAF)
809 North 1500 West
Salt Lake City, UT 84116
Website: http://www.gutenberg.org
Email: help2018@pglaf.org
Facebook: @ProjectGutenberg
Twitter: @gutenberg_org
Project Gutenberg is a volunteer organization that digitizes and
archives historical documents. Its collection includes
more than fifty thousand items, most of which are full-text
public domain books.

Smithsonian Institution (SI)
PO Box 37012
SI Building, Room 153, MRC 010
Washington, DC 20013
(202) 633-1000
http://si.edu
Email: info@si.edu
Facebook, Instagram, and Twitter: @Smithsonian
The Smithsonian Institution is the world's largest research and
education complex. It includes nineteen world-class
museums, galleries, gardens, and a zoo. The Smithsonian
Institution offers many exhibitions and resources about the
American Civil War.

FOR FURTHER READING

Baptiste, Tracey. *The Civil War and Reconstruction Eras*. New York, NY: Britannica Educational Publishing, 2016.

Bauman, Susan. *Black Civil War Soldiers*. New York, NY: Rosen Publishing Group, 2014.

Crompton, Sam. *Georgia During the Civil War*. New York, NY: Rosen Publishing Group, 2018.

Foner, Eric. *The Fiery Trial: Abraham Lincoln and American Slavery*. New York: W. W. Norton & Co, 2010.

Hinton, KaaVonia. *To Preserve the Union: Causes and Effects of the Missouri Compromise*. North Mankato, MN: Capstone Press, 2014.

Hollar, Sherman. *Biographies of the Civil War and Reconstruction*. New York, NY: Rosen Publishing Group, 2013.

Hunt, Laird. *Kind One*. Minneapolis, MN: Coffee House Press, 2012.

Jones, Viola, and Philip Wolny. *A Primary Source Investigation of the Underground Railroad*. New York, NY: Rosen Publishing Group, 2016.

Lanier, Wendy. *What Was the Missouri Compromise?: And Other Questions About the Struggle Over Slavery*. Minneapolis, MN: Lerner Publications, 2012.

Morris, Rob, and Paul Marcello. *The Civil War Close Up*. New York, NY: Rosen Publishing Group, 2016.

Myers, Walter Dean. *Riot*. New York, NY: Egmont USA, 2009.

Swanson, James L. *Chasing Lincoln's Killer: The Search for John Wilkes Booth*. New York, NY: Scholastic Press, 2009.

BBC News. "How Many Soldiers Died in the US Civil War?" April 4, 2012. http://www.bbc.com/news/magazine-17604991.

Berry, Daina Ramey. "Breaking Down the Myths and Misconceptions About Slavery in America." *Newsweek*, June 19, 2017. http://www.newsweek.com/slavery.

Biography.com. "Jefferson Davis." Accessed January 20, 2018. https://www.biography.com/people/jefferson-davis-9267899.

Century Illustrated Monthly Magazine. Vol. 77. Scribner & Company, 1909. p. 920.

Edwin Booth." Biography.com. Accessed January 20, 2018. https://www.biography.com/people/edwin-booth-39624.

Feimster, Crystal N. "Rape and Justice in the Civil War." *New York Times*. https://opinionator.blogs.nytimes.com/2013/04/25/rape-and-justice-in-the-civil-war.

Hamner, Christopher. "The Disaster of Innovation: What Was the Effect of the Cotton Gin on Slaves?" Teaching History. Accessed January 20, 2018. http://teachinghistory.org/history-content/ask-a-historian/24411.

Harriet Tubman Historical Society. "Role in the Civil War." Accessed January 19, 2018. http://www.harriet-tubman.org/role-in-the-civil-war.

History.com. "Freedmen's Bureau." Accessed January 20, 2018. http://www.history.com/topics/black-history/freedmens-bureau.

Klein, Christopher. "10 Things You May Not Know About Abraham Lincoln." *History.com*. Accessed January 19, 2018. https://

www.history.com/news/10-things-you-may-not-know-about
-abraham-lincoln.

Lincoln, Abraham. "Peoria Speech, October 16, 1854." National
Park Service, October 16, 1854. https://www.nps.gov/liho
/learn/historyculture/peoriaspeech.htm.

New York Times, "The Fort Sumter Correspondence." April 29,
1861. https://www.nytimes.com/1861/04/29/archives/the
-fort-sumter-correspondence.html.

NPR. "Lincoln's Evolving Thoughts on Slavery, and Freedom."
NPR.org. Accessed January 19, 2018. https://www.npr
.org/2010/10/11/130489804/lincolns-evolving-thoughts
-on-slavery-and-freedom.

Schulman, Marc. "Economics and the Civil War." History Central,
2015. http://www.historycentral.com/CivilWar/AMERICA
/Economics.html.

Sherman, William T. *The Memoirs of General W.T. Sherman*.
New York, NY: D. Appleton and Company, 1889. Project
Gutenberg, 2006. https://www.gutenberg.org/files/4361/4361
-h/4361-h.htm.

Wakeman, Sarah Rosetta, and Lauren Cook Burgess, ed. *An
Uncommon Soldier: The Civil War Letters of Sarah Rosetta
Wakeman, Alias Private Lyons Wakeman, 153rd Regiment,
New York State Volunteers*. Pasadena, MD: The Minerva
Center, 1994.

Walsh, Colleen. "The Emancipation Proclamation Now." *Harvard
Gazette*, February 4, 2013. https://news.harvard.edu/gazette
/story/2013/02/the-emancipation-proclamation-now.

Wired. "Nov. 15, 1864: Sherman's March to the Sea Changes
Tactical Warfare." Accessed January 20, 2018. https://www
.wired.com/2010/11/1115-sherman-march-to-sea.

INDEX

ABOUT THE AUTHOR

Alana Benson is an author, researcher, and consultant. She has worked extensively with middle school and high school students both in school and in after-school programs. With a dual bachelor's degree in English and classical civilizations from the University of Vermont, Benson is passionate about both reading and history. She has published several titles with Rosen Central, including two health-related titles and another on world history. She is also the author of two books with LexisNexis on identity theft and fraud.

PHOTO CREDITS

Cover Everett Historical/Shutterstock.com; cover banner and interior pages (flags) Enrique Ramos/Shutterstock.com; p. 7 Bryan Hainer/Blend Images/Getty Images; pp. 10, 23 Bettmann /Getty Images; pp. 13, 32, 51 Hero Images/Getty Images; p. 15 Interim Archives/Getty Images; p. 17 Corbis Historical/Getty Images; p. 21 Maskot/Getty Images; p. 26 Blend Images –JGI/Jamie Grill /Brand X Pictures/Getty Images; p. 29 De Agostini Picture Library /Getty Images; p. 34 Steve Debenport/E+/Getty Images; pp. 37, 39 John Parrot/Stocktrek Images/Getty Images; p. 42 Mark Edward Atkinson/Blend Images/Getty Images; p. 45 Buyenlarge /Archive Photos/Getty Images; p. 47 Hulton Archive/Getty Images; p. 53 Dean Mitchell/E+/Getty Images.

Design and Layout: Nicole Russo-Duca; Editor and Photo Researcher: Elizabeth Schmermund